Arthur B. Woodford

The Economic Primer

a summary of the philosophy of lower prices, higher wages and shorter

hours

Arthur B. Woodford

The Economic Primer
a summary of the philosophy of lower prices, higher wages and shorter hours

ISBN/EAN: 9783337239206

Printed in Europe, USA, Canada, Australia, Japan

Cover: Foto ©Suzi / pixelio.de

More available books at **www.hansebooks.com**

THE

[redacted]MIC PRIMER

[redacted]HE PHILOSOPHY OF LOWER
[redacted]IGHER WAGES AND
[redacted]RTER HOURS

[redacted]THUR BURNHAM WOODFORD, Ph.[redacted]
[redacted]nomics and Politics at the School of Social [redacted]

ADVANCE SHEETS

NEW YORK
SCHOOL OF SOCIAL ECONOMICS
34 Union Square

CONTENTS.

Principles of Production.

Principles of Distribution.

Questions of Economic Policy.

On the History of Economic Theory.

CHAPTER I

CHARACTER AND FUNCTION OF
WEALTH

1.—Economic Science.

Social economics is the science of the industrial life
of man. It deals primarily with the material welfare
of mankind, the conditions of well-being in society, and
with the influence of industrial forces upon the mental
and moral development of the race. It deals with human
wants as motives to economic activity; with the means
of getting a living, and with social institutions in so
far as these have an industrial foundation. Social
economics has to do with trade and commerce, with
industrial organization, and the effects of political forms,
of laws, and of moral codes on the industrial condition
of society. It explains changes in agriculture, manufactures and transportation ; fluctuation in prices ; variations in wages; the distribution of population; the
location of industries ; the rights and duties of employer
and employee. It concerns the forms of industrial life,—
slavery, serfdom, the wage system; the kinds of industry,—agriculture, trade, manufactures, transportation ;
the characteristic features of industrial life,—prices,
wages, rent, interest, profits; and the relationships
existing under various systems,—that of slaves and
owners, serfs and masters, employers and employees,
capitalists and wage-earners.

The social economist studies ways of living and
working in society; he investigates the industrial

habits of men and women, groups the facts of human nature, and seeks those lines of uniformity whose statement constitutes a scientific law. For instance, he studies the history of prices, and endeavors to make a generalization concerning the trade experiences of mankind; recognizing that the popular definition of wages, as the price of labor, is truly scientific, he looks to the laws of price for an explanation of all changes and differences in wages,—why wages are ten cents an hour in one place and ten cents a day in another; why the wages of the English agricultural laborer rose from a penny a day in 1300 to 1s. 6d. in 1800 and to nearly 3s. at the present time, while in some parts of Russia, in India, in China, wages are now not over six pence a day; why mechanics in New York City receive as high as five dollars per day and the hod-carrier only two dollars.

The social economist explains why the power-loom superseded the hand-loom and the railroad displaced the stage-coach; why the city street was built upon the country lane; why these changes occur sooner in one country than in another; why slavery still exists, and the reasons for the change from slave conditions to serfdom, and for the still more important change to the wage system.

But all this study is not merely for the comprehension of past changes; the practical result arrived at is the suggestion of new modes of life and that direction of public policy which shall secure rightly and rapidly a still higher type of society in the present and future. The social economist searches for the reasons underlying the constant changes in social and industrial institutions only with a view to their rational perfection.

2.—Man's Relation to Wealth.

No study is of greater importance to the welfare of mankind. The social economist studies the manifold ways

in which man attempts to create wealth,—the thousand
and one devices to economize human life and energy, and
compel the natural forces outside of man to supply the
human family with the means of life and of social com-
fort. Economists investigate the use made of wealth
in the satisfaction of the physical, mental, moral and
social wants—wealth always being regarded as the
most important means to a higher social life.

Whatever may be said of wealth as an end, its existence
marks the difference between civilization and barbarism. A people must remain barbaric without it, however corrupt the abnormal accumulation or uneconomic
use of it may render the nation.

Wealth has been constantly regarded with increased
importance from the beginning of history. Everywhere
and under all conditions man has been seeking for
more wealth. As his individual wants have been increased, either in quantity or quality, so he has constantly required more wealth for their gratification.
Every device has been invented for making nature
yield more of her bounty. Every social condition has
been improved that man may have more to satisfy his
wants, physical, mental and moral. This gives us the
key to our subject; we are to study man seeking
wealth because of the service which it is to him. In
the past the acquisition as well as the consumption of
wealth has been largely empirical and at haphazard.
Social economics can justify itself only by substituting
scientific precision in the economic policy of the
nations of the earth.

3.—Types of Industrial Organization.

Although the changes in industrial and social forms
have been of an almost infinite number, when distinguished by their slight variations and almost insensible
gradations, yet there have been, broadly speaking, but

three distinct types : slavery, serfdom and the wage
system.   As soon as man emerges from a simple,
individual, and largely animal life, in which the sci-
ences of ethnology and anthropology everywhere have
found him, human slavery is to be seen, and has continued as a form of social life down to the present time.
It was the first step from primitive barbarism toward
perfect civilization.   Being of service to a portion, at
least, of mankind, in that it saved labor—the aim and
condition of every industrial advance—it was generally
adopted.   Differing from what precedes, it served to
fill the gap between the nomadic condition and prepare
the way for feudalism and its successor.

A slave is simply property for the service of his owner,
and receives the "reward of labor"—his living—as
does a horse or any other animal.   He is absolutely
the victim of his circumstances, may be bought and
sold, separated from wife, children or place of nativity,
and is without liberty of opinion.   He walks under the
rod, with no opportunity to defend himself against the
power of his master or the less humane overseer.   He
is simply a beast, like them supposed to have no desires
worthy consideration.   He is of value only as he
serves others in obtaining wealth for the gratification
of their wants.   Even this social state is an advance
over the preceding condition.   He is pretty certain of
regular food, suitable clothing and a place to sleep,
with which the master has to supply him in order that
he may be kept in good working order.   The uncertain,
irregular life of the savage has given place to the systematic security of crudely organized, but yet organized, industry.

Serfdom is the next higher, distinct type of industrial
organization.   A serf is bound to his lord's estate and cannot be detached from it.   He is governed by the lord.   His
residence is fixed, but, unlike the slave, what he eats

and wears is determined by his own desires. He may, by his own efforts, live better than any slave. A part at least of his time is his own. He has land which he may cultivate, rights of pasturage for his flocks, and the privilege of gathering fuel on the domain of his manorial lord. In exchange for labor dues, he receives such protection as his lord sees fit to accord.

Under the wage system, man ceases to be attached to other men or to the land. He is no longer a ward, subject to the absolute will of others. Instead, he is the seller, not the sold. Labor and not the laborer is exposed for sale in the market; service and not man is the object of purchase. The wage-earner works not because of a whip held over him by a master, nor because of the exorbitant demands of a lord, but because he has desires of his own which he seeks to gratify. His relation to those for whom he works, to the products of his own labor, and to the community, is altogether different from that of the slave or serf. For his service he may, to an extent, determine the price. He is not dependent upon the bounty or generosity of a lord or master. He is responsible to himself for the support of himself and family. Over his produce he has no control. For the labor he bestows upon it he receives a price previously determined by a definite contract between himself and his employer.

A large part of the workers in the western world are under this wage system; but it is necessary to note that all are not. The bootblack, the independent cobbler, the peddler on the street, the lone farmer who tills his own little plot of ground, the sweater's workers under the roof, are not yet wage-workers.

4.—Fundamental Institutions.

These three types of industrial organization, slavery, serfdom and the wage system, have successively marked the progress of civilization. The change from one to the other has been a slow and gradual evolution; it is "a continuous, progressive change, according to certain laws and by means of resident forces." Each of the lower types, although practically superseded, has left marks upon the social organism not yet cleared away. With the merging of the lower into the higher, of the simpler into the more complex, institutions have been developed, so deeply rooted in human nature, so vital to the industrial organism, that they may be regarded as essential to its very existence,— such as the family, private property, church, state and court.

In the present state of our knowledge the attempt to classify social phenomena is of little scientific value. Sociology has as yet advanced but little beyond a descriptive science. But a working basis or suggestive guide for further study and the comparison of different nations may be found in the following outline :

SOCIAL

INSTITUTIONS	RELATIONS	SCIENCES
Family	Domestic . . .	
State	Civic or Public . .	Politics
Church	Ecclesiastical . .	
Court	Legal	Jurisprudence
School	Educational . .	Pedagogics
	Industrial . . .	Economics
	Intellectual . .	{ Science and Philosophy
	Moral	Ethics
	"Social" . . .	{ Æsthetics "Culture" Linguistics

One marked characteristic of modern life is strong monogamic relations. The social unit is the family of one man and one woman with their children, each and all having more or less clearly defined rights and privileges toward each other and against the rest of mankind.

Almost equally important is the institution of private property, both in the products of man's effort and in the natural agents, over which he has acquired power. For the use of private property the owner may receive rent. For the use of capital the owner may receive interest. For labor or personal service wages must be paid.

Each of these institutions stands on an equality before the law. For the observance of contract relations all parties are equally bound. All contracts must be faithfully kept, for they are the foundation of the whole current of modern business. Indeed, "one may say that modern society rests on the following fundamental ideas: the notion of country, family, liberty, property, civil and political equality in general, labor, faith in contracts freely entered into, obedience to the law and to the powers instituted to guarantee security to society and to each of its members, and, finally, on the ensemble of moral and religious beliefs, which instruct and strengthen the soul, and temper certain suggestions of individual interest with inspiration of equity, of devotion, and of self-denial." *

5.—Divisions of Industry.

Speaking broadly, wealth is produced in three different ways: (1) by agriculture and the extractive industries; (2) by trade, commerce and transportation; and (3) by manufacture, in the common acceptation of the term. To obtain directly from nature the means of satisfying wants, by hunting and fishing, by raising flocks and tilling the soil, is still the industrial method of the larger portion of mankind. But agriculture is by no means the only source of wealth, as was maintained in the middle of the last century by the Physiocrats, a

---

* Jourdan, Cours Analytique d'Economie Politique, p. 297.

school of French economists who went so far in their
revolt against the mercantilists as to regard land as the
only source of wealth, and to limit the term production
to its cultivation, or to its direct use,—as· in mining
and forestry. Every other pursuit was considered
unproductive. Those who labored in the field were
producers; all the rest of mankind were sterile and
unproductive.

Adam Smith (1776) vigorously attacked this idea, and
clearly demonstrated that all the various lines of trade
and commerce are as truly productive as agricultural
efforts. Indeed, they that go down to the sea in ships
often contribute more to the world's well-being than do
the hewers of wood and the drawers of water. Civilization advances with increased speed only with the
development of commerce, manufactures and the artis-
tic industries.

In the primitive community, each individual satisfies
his wants by his own unaided efforts. For food, clothing or shelter he is dependent upon himself alone.
In the family is seen the simplest differentiation; the
man hunts and fishes, the woman toils at home with
cooking and the making of clothes, and possibly culti-
vating the soil a little. Between families barter takes
place in the direct exchange of bows and arrows for
food. Gradually this exchange takes place between
individuals or families separated by some distance.
When neither has time to go to the other, either to
receive or to deliver the articles exchanged, the necessity is developed of a go-between, an intermediary, a
middleman, who receives and delivers the goods.
This, to those immediately interested, is a saving of
time and an economy of effort. Each obtains more
than before. The individuals and the community are
the richer. As Emerson describes the process in his
essay on Wealth, "the art of getting rich consists not

in industry, much less in saving, but in a better order.
. . . Steam is no stronger now than it was a hundred
years ago, but is put to a better use. A clever fellow
cunningly screws on the steampipe to the wheat crop.
The steam puffs and expands as before, but this time it
is dragging all Michigan at its back to hungry New
York and England."

But for the work done by the intermediary, who is
not merely a transporter, but to a certain extent a trader,
those whom he serves must render an equivalent. This
must be sufficient to support him and his family, else
he cannot continue the service. The better order must
be self-sustaining.

Later still the necessity will arise of having some
devote themselves entirely to transportation while
others will confine their work to trade, either wholesale
or retail. At first the trading will be periodic, as at the
great mediæval fairs; but soon it will continue throughout the year. The merchant then becomes a necessity
to the life of the community, and an efficient agent in
production. This further differentiation saves time and
economizes effort. It is not a burden on any individual
in the community, but distinctly contributes to the
wealth and prosperity of all. In the same way is developed the necessity and the utility of the drummer, the
shipper, the banker, all of whom are employed because
they perform a distinct function. So also in time arises
the necessity of soldiers, policemen, lawyers, legislators
and insurers, who by protection, or in other ways,
serve the community. No division will be introduced
and continued unless it is distinctly to the advantage of
those served. Unless the new agents contribute in
some way to the satisfaction of human desires, every
one has an immediate interest in eliminating them from
the industrial body.*

---
* See Gunton's " Principles of Social Economics," p. 63.

6.—Definition of Wealth.

In entering upon the study of wealth and the law and order of its production, the questions to be considered are: (1) What is wealth? (2) Why is it produced? (3) What constitutes production?

In popular phraseology, the word wealth always conveys the idea of an abundance of the things suited to gratify human wants and desires. Unfortunately the term has no uniformly accepted signification even among economists. Yet there are certain characteristics that must distinguish wealth from all other things. We must emphasize the fact that wealth is not a part of man himself, and yet it has no existence separate from man. It is peculiar to him as a social being. It is of service to him, and is created only at his bidding.

We sometimes hear the expression "natural wealth"; but wealth is purely social. Only possibilities, or opportunities, exist in nature. Natural includes whatever exists as the result of purely cosmic forces; but nature is not wealth. Gold in the mine, fish in the sea, the mighty power of Niagara, iron and coal in the mountains of Pennsylvania, all these have existed for ages. The Indians roved over them. But none of these things were wealth until they were touched by the magic of man and made to serve him. The sun, wind and rain are not wealth. They serve man, minister to his needs and satisfy his wants. But they are gratuitous forces, whose services are rendered to man without the expenditure of effort upon his part. If to obtain them he has to work, they become wealth. If he has to explode bombs, as was lately tried in Texas to obtain rain, or erect windmills or spread sails as on ships to obtain motive power, or build light-shafts as in the crowded tenements of the great cities, the product,—moisture, power or light,—is wealth. To call all sunlight wealth

is to break down the line of division between the physical and the social or economic field. It must be necessary to expend human effort in order to put products of
nature into the possession of those whose wants they
are to satisfy, or they are not wealth.

The term wealth includes only those things which
are subject to human control. The falling dew may be
very useful to man in the production of wealth, but
being a result of purely cosmic influence, and not transferable, it is not to be classed as wealth. Honesty is
the best policy, but it is clearly an attribute of human
beings ; it is a personal quality which cannot be transferred and made the subject of a business transaction.
Virtue, intelligence, health, may be higher and better
than wealth ; they may be means to wealth ; but they
are not the thing itself.

Man himself is not wealth unless he is a slave.
Man's mental, moral and physical faculties are not
wealth. They indicate what he is, not what he has.
We shall define wealth, therefore, as any (1) useful
thing (2) outside of man (3) whose utility depends upon
the expenditure of human energy.

This definition will include all things which are the
product of human activities, adapted to the exigencies
of social life, and actually satisfying some human want.
A song, an oration, a sermon, a display of fireworks,
a race, in so far as these are the product of man and
for the service of man, are wealth. Thus it appears
that the degree of duration, or the susceptibility of
accumulation, do not necessarily enter into the definition of wealth. A diamond is no more wealth than a
beautiful song, although the former may be stored
away and outlast many generations, while the latter
gave satisfaction for but a brief moment, and ever after
exists only as a sweet remembrance in the mind of the
hearer. The songs of Patti and Nilsson, the perform-

ances of Shakespeare's immortal dramas by Booth and
Barrett, the noble orations of Curtis, the inspiring utter-
ances of Phillips Brooks, all served man for the brief
moments in which they were being delivered; yet they
were wealth, and much of such wealth is far more
humanizing and socializing in its influence than some
forms of wealth which are susceptible of accumulation
and repeated redistribution.

7.—Production.

Nothing being wealth which does not require the
expenditure of human energy for the creation of its
utility, it is clear that all labor which creates utility is
productive.   To extract raw material from the earth, to
transport it, to change it by process of manufacture
into new forms, to expose it for sale, to insure and
protect it until it reaches the consumer, each and all
are processes of production.   The purpose and the
result is the creation of utility, of things to satisfy
man's wants and desires.   Therefore we say that all
efforts are productive which result, directly or indirectly, in imparting to matter any of the attributes, or
surrounding it with any of the conditions, which make
it available for the gratification of human wants or the
satisfaction of human desires.   Only those efforts are
unproductive and economically useless which fail to
achieve the object for which they were put forth, such
as building a house that no one wants at the price it
cost the owner, working an already exhausted mine,
or sowing seeds in waste places.   These are nonpro-
ductive.   These efforts are misdirected, and fail to
gratify any human desires.

We thus have one supreme industrial test of all
effort.   If we desire to know whether it is productive
or not, we must ask the question, does it gratify a
human want?   From this point of view it will be

clearly seen that much of the effort regarded by some economists as unproductive, is indispensable to the making of many things which are useful to mankind. The farm hand, the workmen on the railroad, the clerks in the bank or the insurance office, the scientist, school-teacher, artist, any and all who contribute the quality of utility to any object, are producers. Moreover, the utility produced by ministers, actors, musicians, serves to gratify a very high order of human desires; indeed, of all kinds of effort they are the most effect-ive in producing the new wants which constitute the incentive to the production of material things. These are as purely economic as those for the gratification of which the farmer raises wheat and wool, or the miller and the manufacturer expend further effort in preparing these materials for consumption. In each instance wants are satisfied. The erroneous idea, so largely prevalent among wage-workers and farmers, that middlemen are non-producers, and that rent, interest and profits are robbery, is the legitimate product of the self-contradictory doctrine that useful effort is non-productive.

Another erroneous notion is that an article must be put on the market and sold, or the effort or service must be paid for in coin, else it is unproductive. A person who makes his own clothes, who raises his own provisions, who paints a picture or plays a musical instrument for his own amusement or that of his friends, is a producer, just as fully as the tailor, or the artist, or the market gardener. Each creates utility and gratifies human desires.*

8.—Necessary Factors in Production.

In the creation of utility it is sometimes taught that man alone does everything, that "labor" is the only

* See Gunton's "Principles of Social Economics," pp. 69-72.

factor in production. Hence the cry that all the price received for anything should go to the laborer, and whatever is withheld, or given to others, is robbery. It is a fact that all production requires labor, and thus cost is imparted to all products. But labor is not the only factor. There are natural forces, such as the air, the heat and the light of the sun, and moisture, which also create utility, and almost always gratuitously. When this is true they add nothing to the cost. But when, in order to obtain the right quantity of air, the necessary degree of heat, the essential amount of moisture, it is necessary to expend labor or invest wealth, then these forces in production add to the cost. Some natural forces, such as steam and electricity, which are so essential to modern processes of production, can never be utilized without the expenditure of effort and the employment of wealth, thus imparting cost. Hence they are never used unless they bring increased returns. Wealth thus employed to assist production is distinguished from that used in consumption, and is called capital.

In addition to labor and capital, land is a necessary factor in production. This is a natural agency, to be sure, but for purely historical reasons must always be separated from those heretofore referred to. We regard as land all wealth invested in and inseparable from land, and the return from it is called rent.

All these three, then, labor, capital, and land, are necessary factors in the simplest, and, as well, in the most complex processes of production. No industrial product can be obtained without a combination of the three, although they are not always equally important in business, and they do not contribute equal amounts of productive force at the same cost. To understand their relations, the principle of their use, the advantages derived from each, the cost which each imparts and the returns which each must receive, are the problems of social economics.

9.—Capital.

We have defined wealth as everything produced by man capable of gratifying human wants. But all wealth is not immediately put to this use; some is set aside for and devoted to the production of other wealth. The wealth thus utilized is capital. Food and clothing, books and paintings, carpets and carriages, every form of wealth actually in use by the consumer, and no wealth is produced until it has reached this point, is consumable wealth. While the want-satisfying power is being added to wealth it is raw material. Wool, for instance, is used in the manufacture of cloth, but it cannot be said to have been consumed until the finished product is actually made use of by the human being whose wants it satisfies. If it is made a part of a machine it becomes capital. All buildings, railroads, ships, and other forms of wealth used in processes of production, are capital. The consumer uses wealth directly for the satisfaction of his wants and desires as a part of the cost of his living; the producer uses wealth, not directly for the satisfaction of his wants and desir but to add want-satisfying qualities to other wealth.

Capital is thus an industrial instrument, a tool whose use is necessitated by the increased demand for the services of reluctant natural forces, without which the modern industrial system could not be carried on for one moment. All capital is wealth, but it is a mistake to speak of a laborer's skill as his capital. Skill is not wealth, but an inseparable attribute of the personality of the individual. It is equally misleading to speak of capital as stored-up labor; labor is human energy and can be stored to a very limited extent only, and then

only in the human being to whom it belongs—never in
any form of wealth. It is precisely because laborers
cannot save their labor from month to month, or sell
this week's service next week, that involuntary idleness has such terrors for them. The failure to use, or
the lack of opportunity to use, today's energy, means
that it is lost forever. We never can use it at a later
time.*

10.—Use of Natural Forces.

There is a limit to the power of the human being,
which renders its use expensive in the processes of
production. To substitute the power of reluctant natural forces for man, to use cosmic instead of human
energy, to exploit nature rather than man, is the es-
sence of industrial progress. This is the function of
capital in the industrial organism. Wherever natural
forces are to be used, capital must be invested ; hence
the two terms are synonymous in industry. The one
cannot share in production except by the use of the
other. Capital becomes thus the servant and the benefactor of the community. It saves labor, reduces cost,
lowers prices, abolishes the poverty and ignorance,
the despotism and superstition which characterize the
hand-labor system, and makes possible the gratification
of more wants and desires, both extensive and inten-
sive. All this increased use of nature makes man
richer.

Electricity would not be cheap for light or power if
it were not for the application of capital. Niagara was
not harnessed and its almost immeasurable power
made to serve man until capital was invested. But
the capital is invested only because of a probability of
profit. Nature must be made to work in such a way that
man may obtain not only the same product for less

* See Gunton's "Wealth and Progress," pp. 17-18.

energy, but a much larger product for the same expenditure, thus yielding increased returns by increasing the ratio of income to expenditure.

11.—The Necessity of an Extending Market.

But the increased production is unnecessary and unprofitable unless the market can be so extended as to consume the increase. If the traditional amount only is to be consumed, the new method will be no more desirable than the old, and will not call forth the investment of capital. Improved methods of production usually require the expenditure of such large amounts of capital that increased consumption and more extensive markets are the condition of their successful use. A modern manufacturer can make in a single day all the pens which the monks of the middle ages could have used. Quills were cheaper for them, but are dearer for us. Then it was books which were dear and men cheap; now the books are cheap and the men dear. But if the number of readers and users of books had not vastly increased, it would still be cheaper to copy them by hand than to manufacture a modern printing-press. Hand labor prevailed in the primitive community and was cheap because of the small market. It still characterizes the industrial organism in partially developed countries like Mexico and South America. In such countries the hand-labor system is cheaper than the capitalistic system. Tallow candles for lighting on a very small scale are cheaper than electricity. Where only a few ride, the primitive jinrikisha is cheaper than the railroad. Rapid transit systems are not perfected in our great cities for the benefit of the aristocracy, but for the great mass of travelers. For the aristocracy, who must have a certain style of exclusiveness, private coaches are still the cheaper. Rapid transit is still unknown in the great

cities of China; there is an immense population, but
few have occasion to ride. Thus we see how, in order
to make use of capital in the harnessing of natural
forces, we must have numerous and increasing wants
to be gratified, which means a constantly extending
market. With such a market reasonably well assured,
capital is not slow to enter into the business of supplying it. Given a demand, and a supply will be forthcoming as soon as it is possible to produce it. Increase
the demand so that it will be profitable to employ natural forces, and capital will at once unite with them,
and utilize them in the productive process. Everywhere and always it is consumption that causes production. Greater demands will be successfully made
on nature only as a result of increased per capita consumption of wealth, and in response to a growing complexity of social desires on the part of an increasingly
large portion of the community.

12.—Importance of Social Wants.

Human desires and wants are to be divided into two
distinct classes, having specific characteristics, modified by quite different influences and occasioning unlike
industrial results. The wants which are mainly directed
to sustaining life are largely supplied by agricultural products, and involve isolating occupations, like farming
and cattle raising. Such wants can only be developed
in quantity to a limited degree in each individual. But
the wants which arise from the quickening influences
of social intercourse, and which are produced and
modified by our intellectual, moral and æsthetic
natures, can be indefinitely increased in number and
extent in each individual, and may consequently multiply much more rapidly than the population. The
objects of social desire are at first luxuries, then com-
forts, and by constant use become the necessities of

life. It is these wants, the products of social intercourse, which furnish the demands for distinctively manufactured products, leading to concentration of population and the adoption of more socializing occupations. It is in the effort to satisfy these desires, and not because of mere additions to populations, that man is forced to use machinery and adopt better methods of production. Here then is the force that calls forth capital.

The use of capital, however, means the displacement of labor. Were this the net result it would be a catastrophe and lead in fact to the defeat of the new method, because each unemployed laborer would cause a diminution in the market. This explains in a measure the inordinate desire for a foreign market. It is thought that this is the only way by which the displaced labor can be used. But there is another natural method of overcoming the difficulty, which is constantly at work, and one which all can assist in furthering. This is making the multiplication of wants more rapid than the increase of men. Labor-saving machinery will not then produce enforced idleness, for the new wants will call for new methods, and will create the conditions of employment for discharged laborers.

Here we see a constant round. Each addition to the wants of an individual means a demand for a larger quantity and a greater variety of products. This means the adoption of new methods. The new methods mean the employment of new laborers and the bringing of new socializing influences to bear upon them, the creation of new wants and so the same round as before. It is peculiarly the higher social wants that contribute to this end. Their development not only makes the use of capital necessary, but socially possible. Their influence is cumulative in producing differentiation of industry and increasing the complexity of economic life. A slight growth in the per capita consumption of the laboring classes involves an immense addition to the market and leads to manufacture on an increasingly larger scale. This results in a lowering of the price and puts the product within the reach of a still larger number of consumers.

The addition of new wants by the laboring classes also raises the standard and the cost of their living, other things remaining the same. Consequently the cost which they impart to the product of their labor is increased. To offset the inevitable demand for higher wages, the capitalist seeks for cheaper methods of production. This means another lowering of prices, so that high wages and low prices may be correlative terms. The incentive to economize labor is strongest where the cost of it is highest, and at the same time here is the greatest opportunity for the successful use of capital.

Thus the economic movement is constantly progressive. Everything is contributing to the increase of social wants and desires. They in turn furnish the very conditions under which man is saved and nature becomes constantly more serviceable. Man is raised in his ability to appreciate life, and in his power to create wealth. Wealth is always coming more into the reach of man; wages are raised; prices are lowered.

13.—Capital the Result of Progress.

The intimate connection between the increase of capital and the progress of civilization leads many to consider that capital is the cause of progress. Capitalists flatter themselves that industrial progress is mainly due to their self-sacrifice and social martyrdom, and that therefore the laboring classes are under eternal obligations to them. Such teachings are as false as the socialist doctrines that the laborer is the sole producer of wealth, and the capitalist an economic robber. Capital is the result of progress rather than its cause. True, it saves labor, but primarily because labor is too expensive, and nature a cheaper workman. Even in the most primitive stages of industry the initial investments are made with a view of securing a greater ultimate amount of pleasure and profit, not indeed for the consumer, but for the capitalist—the producer. Instead of the laborers being indebted to the capitalist for their prosperity, it is just the opposite. It is the extension of the habitual wants of the masses of the community which has made the existence of the capitalist a necessity, and his success possible. And this will always be true.

Nature does the least for man, capital is the least used in the production of wealth, where the social life of the community is least complicated, where wants are the fewest, and where the per capita consumption of wealth is the smallest. There are no capitalists among the Esquimaux, because there is no economic use, no practical need, for capitalists. The social habits of the people are so simple, that they can personally supply their wants with the rudest tools far more cheaply than with the complicated machinery of our civilization.

14.—Parsimony.

Nor is capital the result of abstinence, of self-denial, of "saving," of parsimony, as is so often claimed. Capital comes from production and creation, not from restraint. It is born and invested again in the hope of gain. What great capitalist goes without anything? The multi-millionaires could not by any possibility spend their income in the securing of the satisfaction of their personal wants. The capital invested in the great railroads and other industries is drawn from the profits which are over and above the cost of living of its owners. It is not probable that one per cent of the world's present capital is the result of personal sacrifice.

It is liberality, not parsimony, judicious expenditure and not niggardly scrimping, that promotes social life, increases prosperity and raises the level of civilization. The proverbs of saving which abound in our English language are only half true. Economic literature in its praises of abstinence is equally mistaken. The virtue of having wants and supplying them is ignored. Yet it is just this that makes possible the use of capital and the extension of man's control over nature. Nature will not work cheaply for a few. Factory methods of production did not supplant hand labor until the latter was inadequate to supply the demand for textile fabrics and the other conveniences of life, which are now necessities. The priest was able to copy books more cheaply than could be done by any other method, until the mass of people began to read. It does not pay to invest capital in any industry while the market is small. If, in the olden days, the ruling classes had used their power to develop instead of repress the social desires of the common people, the history of civilization would have been quite different. It is the extension of social wants and desires, not the parsimonious simplicity urged by our fathers, that increases progress. He who creates two wants where there was only one is the greatest benefactor of humanity.

Summary Concerning Wealth.

1. Wealth is anything the utility of which is created by human effort.

2. Capital is wealth used in the creation of other wealth—the tools and machinery required in order to make use of the forces of nature.

3. Natural forces (capital) become cheaper and supplant human energy (labor) in production in proportion as the social wants of the members of the community increase.

CHAPTER II

MONEY, A MEDIUM OF EXCHANGE

15.—The Origin of Money.

In primitive society each individual produces all things necessary for the satisfaction of his own wants. It is only as individuals begin to produce things to satisfy desires of others that trade commences and money be-. comes a necessity. One of the evidences of an advancing civilization is to be found in this differentiation of industries. At first the trade is simply barter,—the direct exchange of commodities between parties each of whom desires what the other possesses more than he desires that which he has in hand.

A farmer desires shoes. He has apples which are less useful to him than shoes, so he seeks a shoemaker who desires the apples, and who will receive them as the economic equivalent of a pair of shoes. This is barter.

But this direct exchange cannot always continue. The farmer and the shoemaker have a variety of wants which necessitate trade with a number of different people. When the people of a community desire to exchange articles for which they cannot give a sufficient quantity of an acceptable commodity, money becomes necessary, and some form of wealth, or promise to pay wealth, comes to be used as a medium of exchange. Under such circumstances what the shoemaker will accept from any one as the economic equivalent of a pair of shoes must be something that he can pass on to

other members of the community and which will be
equally acceptable to all.   This something is money.

Many different articles have thus been used, the teeth
of whales in Fiji, olive oil in the Ionian Islands, dogs by
the Esquimaux, cattle (whence our word pecuniary) by
the Romans, salt in Abyssinia, leather in Carthage, and
tobacco in Virginia.   The catalogue is a long one, consisting of over a hundred different articles, from agate,
amber and bananas to wheat, whiskey, wood and zinc;
it includes beads, shells, tea, tobacco, sheep, slaves,
horses, iron, copper and the precious metals, coined
and uncoined.   In all cases where wealth is used as
money, the trade is still a species of barter, the exchange
of wealth whose value is more or less exactly and generally understood, for other wealth, desired to satisfy
some particular want.

Thus money is the medium of exchange; facilitating
trade and enabling the satisfaction of wants where
there is not a coincidence of desires.   By its use trade
becomes complex, exchanges are extended in time,
future satisfaction is substituted for the immediate, and
credit is utilized without in any way violating the equity
of an economic transaction.   In this way money
becomes the most important institution connected with
the production and exchange of wealth.   It is to industry what blood is to the human body.   Without it, production on an extended scale cannot take place, and
trade beyond the simplest barter is impossible.

16.—The Relation of Money to Wealth.

But pure money is accepted not as wealth, but as a
substitute for wealth.   The shoemaker accepts money
from the farmer in lieu of wealth.   It is of absolutely
no use to him except as he can exchange it for wealth,
and he receives it because wealth cannot then be given.
It is an evidence of debt by means of which he can

obtain from others, at some other time and place, wealth suited to his needs.   A laborer receives two dollars per day.   That is his nominal wages.   He cannot eat it or drink it.   But he can exchange it for food, clothing, shelter, amusement and other forms of wealth.   These are his real wages; these things actually satisfy his desires.   Money is received on the assumption that it will be taken without any discount in the community. Wherever money ceases to be so received in that degree it ceases to be money.   Money is money by virtue of its being current, not because of the property it may contain.   A silver dollar at the present time contains only about fifty-nine cents' worth of silver, yet it is received by all for one hundred cents.   Some seven or eight different kinds of money—"dollars"—are in circulation in the United States for convenience in trade; bronze pennies, nickels and subsidiary silver coins, treasury notes, gold and silver certificates, "greenbacks," and national bank notes, together with checks, drafts, and the promissory notes of individuals and corporations; all pass current in exchange for commodities and for gold coin.   They are received as money. If the pennies and notes were regarded simply as wealth they would not be so accepted.   It is only as money, that is, as a title to wealth as yet not delivered or possibly not created, that they are accepted.   Directly as confidence in them prevails can business be conducted in a progressive society.

In a primitive community wealth must be used as money, because no one can trust any one else and an exact economic equivalent must be delivered at once. The exact reverse is true of a highly civilized society; the promise is at least as good as the reality.   Indeed, the degree of civilization may be inferred from the amount of wealth which a community uses as money. In this respect the United States is ahead of England;

England is ahead of France; France is ahead of Germany, and Germany ahead of other countries.* The use of personal checks is constantly increasing in this country, and the use of coins and other kinds of government money is thus relatively diminished.

Barter money is an evidence of economic insecurity, and of an undeveloped industrial condition. As the moral character of the community rises, and it becomes certain that a man will do as he agrees, the necessity of using wealth for money diminishes. Money is an efficient agent and evidence of progress only as it ceases to be made of wealth and is taken on faith,—as it assumes such form that it is received not for its own sake and for personal use, but exclusively with a view to its being transferred to others in trade.

17.—Functions of Money.

The use of money in facilitating exchanges, in furthering the complexity of trade, in substituting credit for actual wealth, has already been referred to. All these enable the members of a community to secure what they want, when they want it, and in quantities suited to their needs.

But there is another function which money performs, and that is in creating a "common denominative of value," by which the value of different quantities of wealth and service can be measured and compared.

In order to do this successfully money must always have certain important characteristics.†

(1) It must always, whatever its name, form or character, have relation to a specific quantity of a definite kind of some particular article of consumption. In the United States, since 1837, the standard monetary

---

* A secretary of legation is my authority for the statement that enough coin changes hands every three months in Berlin in the payment of house rent to satisfy the needs of New York for a year.

† See Chevalier, La Monnaie, pp. 15-17.

unit, the dollar, has had relation to twenty-five and eight-tenths (25.8) grains of gold nine-tenths fine. In England, since 1816, the standard monetary unit, the pound, has had relation to one hundred and thirteen (113) grains of gold, to which is added one-eleventh of its weight as alloy. .All promises to pay in these countries are, therefore, for dollars or pounds, although few of either are actually transferred as compared with the amount of money used every day in each country in the conduct of business.

(2) The property used as a unit, and to which all money has reference, must possess a utility which is readily estimated by every one. It will inevitably be that which already circulates as barter money among that portion of the community which will not accept paper or credit money alone. The reason for this is very simple. Whoever accepts money in a transaction does so because the commodities at the disposal of the debtor or creditor are such as he does not desire for his own use or production. So long as the money will be accepted by those who do possess the commodities, it is unimportant what commodity it represents. But when it will not be accepted, it is necessary that the holder should be able to demand from those who issue the promise a specific kind of property, which those who declined to receive his money will accept. Otherwise commercial dealings will be restricted to the limited area in which money freely circulates. So long, therefore, as we have commercial intercourse with any people who continue to insist upon barter money, or a large portion of the community are distrustful of those with whom they have business relations, all money must be promises to deliver upon demand a specific quantity of the commodity of which barter money is made.

(3) As society advances, the articles of which money is made must contain an ever larger value in a small

compass. It must have a high specific gravity industrially. Where wages are low, large coins of little value
can be circulated. But where wages are high, coins of
small size must have great value. Where wages are
six cents a day, few people have use of a gold eagle, for
it would contain what was to them a fortune.

(4) It must be as nearly as possible unalterable in
form and of such durability that its value will not
deteriorate.

(5) It should be of uniform quality and readily divis-
ible, so that every unit will be the equal of every other.

(6) Every form of money should be such that it can
be readily recognized, and counterfeits or similar articles quickly detected.

(7) Above all, the monetary unit must be as free as
possible from variations in value. Articles whose cost
of production depends upon the season, or the process
of whose manufacture is constantly changing, are unfit
for a standard.

Only the precious metals sufficiently combine all
these qualities to constitute a good circulating medium.
Useful, expensive, durable, homogeneous, readily recognized and possessing a fair decree of stability of
value, they are the money materials of the world. Convenience of form is secured by coinage, what it shall
be depending entirely upon the stage of industrial
development the community has attained.

A coin, however, is nothing more than a manufactured commodity; it is wealth, the weight and fineness
being certified by the stamp. As part of the money of
a civilized community, coins are a relic of barbarism.
They show that a portion of the community is not yet
up to that moral standard where barter money can be
dispensed with. Instead of being the only form of real
money, as some people regard them, coins of full
weight and fineness perform the least important func-

tion of money. A metallic currency is entirely inadequate to meet the demands of modern trade and commerce. To be forced to an actual transfer of metal for each exchange would paralyze the commerce of the world. In fact, only three per cent of clearings and less than one per cent of debts are paid in coin; while less than five per cent of debts are settled by using legal tender. It is sufficiently burdensome to carry a little change.

18.—The Money Function of Banks.

The real money of civilized society is the so-called paper money, the difference between it and metallic currency being that the latter is both wealth and money while the former is only money;—it is the promise of wealth. Ricardo has well said that currency is in its most perfect state when it consists wholly of paper.* But that it be perfect, there must exist perfect confidence that currency can be exchanged for any form of property, including barter money, at the pleasure of the holders. It is the prime requisite of promises that they be kept absolutely. So far as money is concerned, this implies that all notes be absolutely convertible at all times. Any monetary system which does not secure this is uneconomic. One which makes notes nothing more than certificates of deposit, like warehouse receipts, is entirely insufficient. In such money there is no economy save in the prevention of abrasion of the coin. It is for these reasons that money must be issued by individuals and by corporations, not by governments.

The work of the early banks was to offer security for property against highway robbers, a function in which the safe-deposit companies have superseded the wayside inn. A second duty was to facilitate exchanges

* Works of David Ricardo (McCulloch's Edition), page 218.

by balancing credits, a work which has reached its
highest development in a clearing house where the
claims held by different banks, amounting to hundreds
of millions daily, can be exchanged in less than ten
minutes and are settled by the payment of only small
amounts of legal tender. The third, and today the
important feature of the banking business, is to lend
and borrow capital,—the savings banks on more perma-
ment forms of property and for longer periods, the
banks of loan and discount on short time, and almost
entirely on goods in transit from the farm and the factory to the point of consumption. Behind the promise
of the latter banks lies the largest mountain of wealth
and the strongest impulse to the creation of more
wealth which exists in the community. Behind the
promise of the fiat of the government rests only the
clumsy power of taxation, the exercise of which cannot
immediately add to the industrial power of the nation.
Governments are manifestly incapable of performing
the task of supplying all the money business men must
use, nor does the treatment afforded its creditors by our
own government warrant the conclusion that perfect
confidence can be reposed in the absolute convertibility
of its promises to pay dollars on demand. The banking system with a central bank of redemption and government supervision to insure the maintenance of a
legal reserve may be expected to afford a safe system
of note issues in the future as it has in the past.*

19.—Advantages of Personal Money.

In the earlier stages of society the government supplied all the money,—the barons in the middle ages,
and the kings and emperors later. But with the development of commerce since the sixteenth century, and

---

*See "Path to Safe Banking and Currency," in the SOCIAL ECONOMIST for
October, 1893.

the extension of manufactures in the nineteenth, the
requirements of business have become too delicate and
intricate for monarchs to control it.   Public money or
legal tender must be supplemented, though not sup-
planted, by private money.   It is probable that governments will continue to supply, under absolute monop-
oly, the token coins and small bills used in retail trade,
and to do the actual work of coining with better results
than we could expect from "absolute free trade in
currency." But the right to have wealth made into
money, as in the free coinage of gold under our present
system, will remain with the the individual citizen and
with the corporation.   Every man in business will also
have the same right he now has to make and issue
money, the only law restraining him being that his
money shall not be made in imitation of that already
in use by some one else, whether it be the government
(counterfeiting) or a private individual (forgery). Thus
may be supplied all that is required for the conduct of
business.

The quantity of legal tender money required in a
highly complex industrial community is subject to sud-
den and extreme variations.   A change in the ratio of
exports to imports ; an increase or decrease in the
movement toward opening up new territory ; a change
in our industrial relations with people who insist upon
barter money exclusively ;—all affect the quantity of
legal tender money required.   The quick decision, ex-
pert judgment and alertness necessary to adapt the
currency to these ever-increasing variations, are precisely what individual enterprise can supply.

The government must act either upon a general rule
or according to specific legislation : it cannot vary its
action with sufficient promptness to meet the varying
requirements of special emergencies necessarily arising
in modern society.   A stringency may arise, or even a

panic, which will, before Congress can be called together, disturb the industrial relations of the whole country. Moreover, political considerations, rather than economic, are likely to have weight in the deliberations of a legislative body. All that is necessary in order to insure the ready adaptation of supply to demand is to have money furnished by private enterprise exactly in the same way that food, clothing, and other commodities are now, with the exception that the form and quality of the money shall be determined by law.

This would involve government control or supervision of the mint and of the printing of coin certificates; but money would really be furnished purely as a matter of business, and bankers sustain the same economic relations to the community as do all other merchants. They would increase their stock in the same way and for the same reasons that shoe merchants increase their stocks of shoes. Being responsible for the supply of barter money, bankers would lose their business, or succeed, according to the efficiency with which they supplied the monetary wants of the community.

This change in our monetary system would take the gold and silver industries out of politics. Instead of lobbying in Congress to increase the market for, and fix the price of, their product, men interested in these industries would go into the open market on the same terms as other producers. The effect of this on these industries can hardly be overestimated. It would also take the whole question of the supply of money out of the field of political action and make it automatic, by leaving it to the action of economic forces and subject to economic law rather than statutes. We should thus obtain in our monetary system all the advantages of competition, business enterprise and skill, without the risk of adulterations and "tricks of the trade." We

should derive all the benefits of the exercise of the pro-
tective power of the state without the bungling incom-
petency inseparable from the public administration of
industrial undertakings.

20.—A " Bimetallism " which is Possible.

Furthermore, the plan here proposed offers a means
of settling the bimetallic controversy.   Until a community advances beyond the barter-money stage of
industry the question of the value of its money is of
little consequence, because the variations must be in-
significant.   But when real money comes to be used,
when the larger part of the money work is done by
credit instruments, and the promise of wealth is taken in
trade instead of the wealth itself, the value of the monetary unit becomes a matter of vital importance.   Slight
variations may involve the welfare of thousands upon
thousands of the population.

As society develops, it becomes necessary to substitute the more for the less expensive monetary article,
and this change is likely to entail some variation in the
monetary unit.   Today some countries can only use
silver, while others must use gold, in part at least ;
when trade is carried on between countries using different money materials because of their being un-
equally developed industrially, successful business requires a stable par of exchange.   It is this that gives
special importance to our silver question.   But thus far
every scheme adopted for using two metals, under free
coinage of both, has been unsuccessful because based
upon the idea of keeping their relative values together
by a fixed ratio of their quantity.   Their respective
values vary, however, because their costs of production
vary.   In the ninth century the proportion in which
the two metals were of equal value was about 9 of silver to 1 of gold ; under the Tudors, the ratio reached

12 to 1 ; during the first three-quarters of this century
it fluctuated between 15 to 1 and 16 to 1 ; in 1892 it was
22 to 1 ; the present market ratio (October, 1894) is
about 30 to 1. Clearly the free coinage of both metals
by any government (national bimetallism) will not
establish a permanent parity of value between them, as
it can have no reference to the relative cost of production which determines the value of each. Whether it
would be possible to establish a parity of value between
them at any fixed ratio of quantity if all commercial
nations were to agree on the ratio (international bimetallism), is, to say the least, doubtful, the experience of many countries for centuries showing that the
values of a given quantity of two metals will not keep
together for any considerable time.

The currency experiences of the sixteenth century
led Sir Thomas Gresham, financial agent of the English
court at Antwerp, to formulate the economic law which
has since borne his name—"bad money drives out
good money." That is, if two kinds of money are de-
clared by authority to be of equal legal value, the one
having the lower cost of production drives the other
out of circulation as soon as the difference in cost becomes apparent.

A fixed ratio of quantity will necessarily give a varying ratio of value unless the margin of variation is
small. It therefore becomes necessary to change the
point of adjustment from quantity to value, if bimetallism is to be rendered possible. Instead of being coined
in a ratio of quantity, metals must be coined in the
ratio of value. Every silver dollar should be the economic equivalent of a gold dollar, without reference to
the number of grains it contains. Instead of trying to
perform the miracle of adjusting the value to the grains,
we must reverse the process, and adjust the grains to
the value. If every coin, of whatever metal, is equal

in value to every other coin of the same denomination, then all reason for restricting the quantity will have disappeared, and coinage can be free.

But little silver need actually be coined, however. Our own recent experience has shown that the silver dollar, like the gold dollar, is an inconvenient coin. All that is necessary is to have every silver certificate represent a dollar's worth of silver. This can be accomplished in the same manner as investors are compelled to keep up their "margin" with brokers. The price of silver does not fluctuate so rapidly that frequent changes in the deposit made by issuers of currency would be necessary. It would have to be immediately increased when the price of silver falls, in order to make the margin good. If more currency is desired, a new deposit would also have to be made. The banker would purchase more bullion and have it coined, or certificates issued, just as the shoe dealer increases his stock when the demand arises. In this way silver can be coined as freely as gold, for the same reasons, and with as much safety. Perhaps the greatest advantage in favor of this change in our monetary system is that it can be adopted in this country irrespective of the action of the rest of the world. We should have a monetary system in which in truth every dollar issued would be of the same value as every other dollar, not only as money, but also as bullion property, the world over.

21.—The Demand for Cheap Money.

It is commonly believed that it is for the interest of the community to have money "cheap." This entirely erroneous notion arises from confounding money with the capital that business men lend and borrow, and also from confusing the character of money with the nature of the wealth materials of which barter money has at times been made. The community is most deeply interested in having wealth cheap; but as money is only the instrument used in exchanging wealth and service, which latter it is for the interest of the vast majority of the community to have dear, and is the measure of the ratio of exchange, every member of society has most concern in having the value of money as stationary as possible. Good money is that which is convenient in form and stable in value. The greater the stability in the value of money the more certain will be the equity of all exchanges, other things being equal.

When the economic effect of a change in the value of money is equally distributed throughout all parts of the industrial body, no one can have the slightest profit therefrom; when the incidence of the impulse is unequal, a temporary interest is created. Creditors, or debtors, then hope to gain what some one else loses,—a gain resembling in character the result of theft. No permanent and economically self-perpetuating interest is created. Farmers and laborers are, moreover, more likely to suffer from these variations, and are most interested in invariability in the value of money, as its efficiency, like that of weights and other measures used in trade, depends upon stability of character. Every one wants to know at all times just how much it is. Only mere money speculators can have an interest in promoting fluctuations in the value of money.

A rise in the value of money, or a fall, may result from a change in the cost of obtaining the money material or from an arbitrary political action. Money falls in value when new mines are discovered, as in California and Australia or Colorado; it depreciates when confidence in the solvency of the issuer is weakened. Money is debased when the government unjustly diminishes the weight of the coin, as did Henry VIII,*

* See Section 42, Chap. IV.

so that it does not represent the property which it pretends to.   An honest money-maker, like the mint of the United States, is necessary in order to prevent the decline through debasement.   Commercial integrity and absolute convertibility at all times will alone secure the confidence which hinders depreciation.

Summary Concerning Money.

1. Coins are a form of wealth, the degree of civilization of any community being indicated by the extent to which it has dispensed with their use.

2. Money is a non-interest-bearing obligation which passes current in the community at its face value in exchange for wealth and service.

3. Money always has relation to a specific quantity of a definite kind of some particular commodity.   This can be best determined by the government.

4. Deposit banks doing a loan and discount business are best equipped for making sound money and determining the quantity needed.   Under proper regulations as to reserve and redemption they can readily adapt the supply of money to the industrial demand.

5. Intelligent currency reform must be directed toward limiting the fluctuations in the value of the money unit or toward increasing the convenience of its forms.

6. No bimetallism is possible which does not secure the equality of value in the various forms of the monetary unit.

CHAPTER III

ON THE LAW OF PRICES

22.—Definition of Value.

Value is ratio of exchange ;—simply that and nothing more. In a broad sense, and the truest, it is the ratio in which man is obliged to give his services in exchange for wealth,—the social ratio of labor to gratification. In a narrower and the more common use of the term, it is the ratio in which quantities of commodities are exchanged. This latter kind of exchange is only the means to the end : various quantities of the different forms of wealth are nominally and directly the subject of trade, but in the last analysis trading is giving labor for the material things required to satisfy our physical, mental, and social desires.

The products of industry have value only because and so long as some one is willing to give wealth or service in exchange for their possession. In order, therefore, that any particular article have value, (1) it must be useful; (2) its utility must depend on the expenditure of human effort, and not on the bounty of nature ; and (3) the article must be transferable, in law and in fact. No one will consciously give anything for an article that is gratuitously supplied in nature and may be had for nothing, nor will people pay for something which they cannot really possess, of which the legal institutions of the community do not guarantee ownership.

When effort is required to obtain useful things, it is put forth, and the thing acquired has value, primarily because the product of the effort is useful. No one continues to give anything voluntarily in exchange for something which will be of no use in the satisfaction of desire. Rather efforts are expended exactly in proportion as we think the resulting wealth will be useful. Consequently nothing can have great value, that is, have such qualities that its owner will be able to exchange it at a high ratio per quantity, except as it has utility in a corresponding degree. Utility may be much greater than value, but it must at least equal value. Men and women do not work hard and long for that which satisfieth not.

Things are dear or cheap at any given time and place according as a particular laborer must work a longer or shorter time to acquire them, that is, according to the ratio in which they will exchange for labor of a given quality. Certain things may be dear at fifty cents apiece in Mexico because wages are only twenty-five cents a day, but cheap at two dollars in the United States, where wages are two dollars and a half or three dollars a day. When it is said that the price of a commodity has risen or fallen, it is implied that a larger or smaller quantity of money is required in exchange; but this statement has no social significance save as it means that it has become more or less difficult for man to obtain the commodity. Wheat cannot become dear to potatoes for the reason that wheat is neither produced, nor bought, by potatoes. Wheat may be compared with potatoes, but it has no exchange relation to them because exchanges are always made by man and for man, with a view to the gratification of some desire, since he must directly or indirectly render some

service to obtain wealth.   His labor must ever be the
ultimate standard of value, the unit by which are determined the ratios at which commodities exchange.

23.—Difference Between Value and Utility.

There are many useful things for which, under ordi-
nary circumstances, man is not obliged to work, such as
air and sunlight. , These are gratuitous means of gratifying his desires, and, as every one has them, no one will
give anything in exchange for them ; they can have no
value.   There is thus a fundamental difference between
value and utility.   The one is a quality of things
which makes it desirable to possess them for their own
sake ; they are useful.   The other is not an inherent
quality of articles, but the exchange relation between
them—a ratio that varies with time and place.   There
can be no such thing, therefore, as "intrinsic" value; it
is a scientific absurdity.   A single thing can have value
only by comparison with other things and with man.
An ounce of gold can no more have value in and of
itself, than the number thirteen can have ratio.   Nor
can a particular commodity have value to an individual.
Value is ratio of exchange, and it takes at least two to
make a bargain. We speak metaphorically of the value of
pure air, of friendship, of adversity, of rest as a restora-
tive, or of the value to health of a perfectly calm and
regular life.   But we invariably mean the utility of each
of these, the word always referring to the direct or the
indirect want-gratifying qualities of some portion of
man's environment.   This quality has a purely personal
significance.   Each individual decides for himself how
useful pure air or a friend may be, and whether they
are worth the effort necessary to obtain them.   Indeed,
only the individual can determine utilities.   Value is
social.   It is the vital impulse of societary circulation,
the extent of the latter marking the difference between

civilization and savagery and showing how far man is removed from Robinson Crusoe conditions.

24.—Relation of Value to Wealth.

Value, moreover, is a simple economic concept; there are not several kinds. Different degrees of value may exist, and the value of particular articles, as well as of commodities in general, be different at different times and in different places. But value is ever and always the ratio at which portions of wealth are exchanged directly for each other and indirectly for service. Value in use, value in exchange, natural value, normal value, market value, commercial value, use value, subjective value, objective value, are either unnecessary or incorrect attempts to modify the simple idea conveyed in the word value, and result in confounding value with utility, or with wealth. Wealth is the thing to be exchanged; value is the ratio in which a given quantity of wealth has exchanged, or is likely to be exchanged, for other wealth, or for service,—a mental estimate only of economic exchange relations.

So unlike are wealth and value that it is the aim of society to increase the one and decrease the other. The welfare of the race is advanced only as wealth in general becomes more abundant and cheaper; as it exchanges for a smaller quantity of human effort, and its value declines. That labor is useful to humanity which increases the wealth of the community. It is of no use to society to increase value. No one desires books, clothes or food to become more expensive. No one wants new machines which raise the cost of production. Progress comes only with the fall in the value of all commodities as measured in human energy or service. Communities are rich in the quantity of good things, not in their relation to each other ; in wealth, not value. If we had twice as much wealth

in the United States as at present, but it were twice as
valuable, we would be no better off. We should have
to work just as hard in proportion to the return obtained
from our industry. In order to progress socially we
must be able to get more wealth with the same effort
or the same wealth by less work. Society progresses
as wealth increases and value diminishes. This is
possible only when through the use of machinery nature
is forced to do a larger share of the work of creating
social utilities. The alternative for individuals, as for
nations, is making some one else labor for us, and that
results either in robbery or slavery: it is not a step
toward a higher civilization.

25.—The Basis of Economic Equivalence.

The law of prices involves the principle on which
rests the equity of all human relations. If every one
could secure the equivalent of all he gives in church
and state, in public and private life, in the family and
the school, in trade and in society, injustice would be
eliminated from human life and an absolutely equitable
reward received for human activities. Speculation
plays such an important part in the production as well
as the societary circulation of goods; such prominence is
given to the dishonesty of retail traders and to the gam-
bling methods of men who cheat the innocent property
holder of at least a portion of the value of his title ; such
strenuous efforts are made to get something for nothing
in our dealings with our fellow men and women, that
we are quite apt to lose sight of the real nature of trade
as in truth an exchange of economic equivalents.

As already explained (Sec. 15), trade implies two
simultaneous equations of two variables. Each boy
offering to swap knives thinks he will be better off—be
placed in a better economic condition by the trade ;
that the ratio of cost to satisfaction will be less as a

result of the exchange. Nor can trade long continue, and hence be an economic exchange and a social fact for the scientific investigator to consider, unless each buyer and seller gains by the transaction and actually receives the economic equivalent for what he gives. Exchanges in which one gains only what another loses, as in all betting, are highly uneconomic and tend to extinguish themselves by reason of the harm they inflict on all concerned. It is only the sales which tend to perpetuate themselves, because they promote general industrial and social well-being that indicate the real character of trade. In these exchanges wealth is created because an increase of utility results from the transfer of ownership; each trader thinks that what he receives will be of more service to him in the satisfaction of his wants than what he gives, and each will continue to trade in a given way because, under the conditions of life and industry which prevail in the community of which they are members, the balance of pain and pleasure, of cost and satisfaction, is best maintained in this process of exchange. If a man sells a farm of a thousand acres for a city lot having only a few feet frontage, he does so because the city lot will satisfy more of his wants than the farm will, or more completely satisfy the same wants. If a man sells a pair of shoes for a hat, or a dozen bushels of wheat for a suit of clothes, or fifty tons of coal for a piano, he does so because for him the hat or the clothes or the piano possesses greater utility. Some one else buys the shoes or the wheat or the coal because these articles are more useful to him, in the light of the effort he must put forth to get them. Each compares cost and satisfaction in the different lines. Everywhere mankind is at work on this problem of comparing cost with returns, pain with pleasure. Ever-varying answers are given to this question by different portions of humanity as the years go by, and as a consequence, people move from place to place, or transfer their labor and capital from one industry to another. The result of this universal movement is to make the value or price of all commodities equal to their cost by making the ratio of effort to satisfaction identical in the various branches of industry. In the long run, this reduces trade to an exchange of economic equivalents.

26.—Value and Price Tend to Equal the Cost.

It is common to conceive of all wealth as being exchanged for money, and hence to speak of price as the amount of money one would like to get in exchange, or as the money value. But practically the value of anything is its price. There is absolutely no difference between these terms. Price, like value, expresses ratio of exchange and nothing else. Nothing is worth more nor less than its price. This price may vary from time to time, but there is a constant tendency to establish one price for each commodity in each market. The constant higgling in a free market brings buyers and sellers to a common point, above which no buyer is willing to buy, below which no seller is willing to sell.

In the instances in which there appears to be more than one price for the same thing in a given market, it is clear that the conditions do not exist for free economic exchange. This manifests itself particularly in the retail trade. Here ignorance is greatest alike as to the quantity, quality, and cost of the article received. The ignorance and poverty of the average consumer make it possible to impose on him. He may be under pecuniary obligation to the dealer or "in the habit of trading" with him, either of which relations creates an uneconomic condition, since it implies ignorance of the conditions under which the trade is taking place, or prevents action in accordance with knowledge.

If we assume that every one in the field of exchange is adequately informed as to the quantity, quality, and other conditions affecting the article which is the object of purchase and sale; that it is an article which is not in a large measure influenced by cosmic forces; that fraud and the numerous devices by which buyer or seller can get a dishonest advantage over the other have been eliminated; that all are free to seek their best interests;—in a word, if we assume well-informed self-interest acting freely, it is invariably true that the price of any commodity tends to equal the cost of its production. Less than this the producer cannot regularly receive. More than this an intelligent consumer will not give.

Under the simplest conditions of human existence man lives on the spontaneous fruits of the earth. His first demand is for game, but it is only after oft-repeated experiences have taught man that the bow and arrow will aid in the gratification of this desire that he feels the demand for a weapon and expends effort in procuring one. The implements of war and the chase will not be produced for market, however, until the price offered makes it more profitable to manufacture them than to hunt for a living. The same is true in modern society, where industry is most complex and labor most highly specialized, and where production is almost entirely for others, each receiving through exchange what he or she consumes. Nothing is regularly produced for which the consumer does not stand ready to give an economic equivalent, because cost is a minimum price which farmer, manufacturer, trader, and every other producer must receive. He cannot constantly sell below cost. To maintain that he can, is to hold that in economics perpetual motion is possible, and that something can be made out of nothing. To sell at less than cost indefinitely is to invite bankruptcy, a course which people do not voluntarily pursue. It is true that a number of considerations may induce a merchant to sell particular articles below cost for a time, and even to part with everything he has at the moment below what it has cost him. He may have miscalculated the necessary cost of handling. He may not know the exact cost of reproducing or replacing the commodities in question. The cost may have changed between purchase and sale. He may be unexpectedly crowded by indebtedness previously incurred and forced to realize immediately. He may have over-estimated the market demand, or he may be using the commodity as a "leader" to attract customers for other goods. But it will be observed in all of these instances that changes in price are not due to permanent economic influences. They are the result of uneconomic perturbations and are merely temporary fluctuations from the economic price level. One gets more and the other less than an equivalent in these particular instances. No merchant or manufacturer can continuously sell everything below cost, without in truth "giving away" his goods.

Will the consumer give more than cost? Equity clearly requires that he should not. And there are economic forces operating automatically to insure that he will not give even the "customary" rate of profit. Under the assumption of freedom of economic action the manufacturer can cease making one commodity and devote his energies to work in other lines whenever the price, by falling below the cost of production, ceases to be an economic equivalent. Under the same hypothetical condition the consumer will refuse to give his money, his services or his commodities in exchange, and will become a producer of the particular article when the present manufacturer demands more than an economic equivalent,—more, that is, than will

afford him as much gratification as he could otherwise
have obtained. This does not mean that the utility of
the two articles is the same for different individuals.
Indeed, utility varies infinitely according to the tastes,
temperament, and idiosyncrasies of different people.
Economic equivalence depends on equality in the
amount of reluctant productive energy expended. Each
compares cost and satisfaction in different lines, and all
the power the producer has, in simple industry, to prevent the price of any article from falling below its cost of
production, the consumer has in an equal degree to prevent its rising above that cost. If he knows the market,
can change his business, and is disposed to seek his
own best interest, the consumer can force the price
down to, but not below, cost; producers cannot force it
above the cost. Exchange can regularly take place at
this point only, because here all exchanges are mutually
advantageous and economic, tending to perpetuate
themselves by the unconscious operation of the forces
in society set in motion by intelligent self-interest.
Through the exchange of commodities in the ratio of
their costs of production, every one obtains an increased utility by giving an economic equivalent, and
by gratifying the desires of others. ·

27.—The Effect of Competition.

Competition, or business rivalry, is the economic
force which tends to make price equal cost, and insures
in the long run that commodities will exchange in the
ratio of their costs of production. In simple economic
conditions and in undeveloped primitive communities
this industrial movement is confined to the competition
of buyers, is not active and perfect, and hence trade is
not equitable. In its crudest form this competition is
the "higgling of the market" where a laborer offers to
buy second-hand clothing in the city street, or the

farmer desires to trade out his butter and eggs at the country store; it is the direct barter of simple, homogeneous society. It leads men to shave themselves, do their own cobbling, and slaughter the beef on the farm.

But as society advances competition is transferred almost entirely to producers, for the reason that buyers cannot readily change their occupation but can readily change their place for trading. It becomes more perfect, however, and reduces trade more accurately to an exchange of equivalents. As the circulation increases in volume and complexity, economic movement becomes more instantaneous and automatic, and greater equity is attained. Competition has its more perfect work in reducing price to cost by distributing profits, which is its only true and efficient economic function.

28.—Analysis of Cost of Production.

It is not what a particular article has cost its present owner that fixes its price, save when it represents what will have to be spent to replace it. Labor and capital once spent in the production of an article have little to do with its value. It is the amount of effort necessary to place another equally satisfactory article on the market that fixes what can be obtained for it in exchange. This can always be reduced to labor cost. In every instance value is made up of three items: cost of labor, cost of raw materials, and cost of tools; but, since each of latter two can again be resolved into three parts as long as either enters into the process of production, in the last analysis it will be found that labor cost is all that remains.

In order that laborers may be able continuously to supply their productive energy, they must regularly receive from an enterprise as much as they have put into it; their wages must equal the cost of living of them-

selves and their families.   It is absolutely impossible
for the employer to obtain the service of a laborer continuously for lower wages than will afford him a living.
A given amount of effort involves a definite cost to the
laborer, and he cannot continue to render the service
unless in return he receives this cost.   The same is
true of the raw material and tools in the hands of the
manufacturer.   He must obtain from the product enough
to equal the wear and tear of the machinery and the cost
of raw materials, for otherwise the one will soon dis-
appear and the other not be brought to market.   Labor,
land, capital and the industrial enterprise required in
organization are each and all requisite to the production of wealth.   The owner of each must receive from
the product the equivalent of what he contributes to
the product.   Nor can he obtain more; all are governed
by the same law.   In the simple conditions where all
laborers are about alike, land is equally poor, and capital easily acquired, there the redistribution of labor and
capital is easy because costs are uniform, and it is clear
the laborer will get what it costs him to live, the land-
lord only the cost of utilizing the land, the capitalist the
equivalent of the cost of what he contributes, and the
manager of an enterprise his living, for the work of
superintendence.   It is only when differential costs
arise that laborers can save, landlords obtain rent, capitalists secure interest, and business men reap profits.

29.—Differential Costs.

As society develops and industry becomes more
highly specialized, costs cease to be uniform.   Almost
no commodities are regularly produced for the market
at a uniform cost for the whole supply, and very few
ever have been.   In the manufacture of cotton cloth,
for instance, there are probably differences of half a
cent a yard in the costs of production in the different

mills in eastern Massachusetts, due to differences in method, in location of plant, quantity of capital, quality of machinery, or in any one of a large number of particulars which distinguish one factory from another.

Everywhere in modern industry there are differential costs, and under the influence of competition among producers, price tends to equal cost in the dearest factory. The following diagram is designed to illustrate the relation of cost to price:

GROUPS OF MANUFAC- TURERS.	PRICE OF PRODUCT.	ACTUAL COST OF PRODUCTION.	PROFIT PER YARD.	
A	3 cents.	$2\frac{11}{16}$ cents.	$\frac{5}{16}$ cent.	Minimum cost.
B	"	$2\frac{3}{4}$ "	$\frac{1}{4}$ "	
C	"	$2\frac{13}{16}$ "	$\frac{3}{16}$ "	
D	"	$2\frac{7}{8}$ "	$\frac{1}{8}$ "	
E	"	$2\frac{15}{16}$ "	$\frac{1}{16}$ "	
F	"	3 "	o "	Maximum cost.

The manufacturers of each group pay the same rate of wages ($2), and sell at the uniform price, which equals the cost of production in the least efficient group of men in the business. So long as the manufacturers of this group (F) remain in the market they must receive their cost of production in the price of the finished product, and all the others will obtain the same, deriving their profit from their superior economic efficiency The other manufacturers could afford to take less, but all together they do not produce the amount of cotton cloth the community stands ready to pay for at the greatest cost. The product of group F is "necessary." The manufacturer in group F gives and receives exactly *quid pro quo*, and has no profit,—his living being part of necessary cost. The other five give the same equivalent, but have a surplus equal to the amount by which they are able to reduce the cost of production below that of the price-fixing group of manufacturers. This is perfectly equitable, because it comes from making nature do the work, and not by robbery of the laborers, as socialists maintain.

GROUPS OF LABORERS.	WAGES.	ACTUAL COST OF LIVING.	SAVINGS PER DAY.	
A	$2.00	$2.00	0 cents.	Maximum cost.
B	"	1.95	5 "	
C	"	1.90	10 "	
D	"	1.85	15 "	
E	"	1.80	20 "	
F	"	1.75	25 "	Minimum cost.

The same principle applies to wages, the price paid for labor. (See diagram.) All laborers receive what those demand who live most expensively. If these are employed they must have the cost of their living, and what they must have all others can get, quite irrespective of their own cost of living. The laborers who live most expensively thus come into contact and contest with the least efficient employers. In a certain sense, laborers in group A represent the community and the interest of consumers. They personify demand seeking a supply for its wants. It is their common interest to lower the maximum cost and thus make possible either lower prices, higher wages, or both. This is illustrated in the cotton manufacturing industry, for example; there wages have risen 100 per cent in England and 115 per cent in this country during the century; prices have fallen from thirty cents a yard to less than three, and the business has remained profitable, although the individual high-profit manufacturer has been lowered seven successive times to the position of no-profit entrepeneur. Progress thus consists in raising the wages of the most expensive laborers and lowering the maximum cost to producers by repeated drafts on the storehouse of nature.

30.—Sequence of Price Phenomena.

The word price has been used as referring to general industrial conditions—as signifying the level toward which temporary fluctuations in prices tend to gravitate, and not the result of some special sale. The price of wheat, speaking generally, is the ratio at which it exchanges on some central market, like New York, Chicago or Liverpool, throughout a considerable period of time— not on a particular day in midwinter or at a small interior town in Russia. Society is not interested in the prices at auction sales, except to eliminate them, but in the usual exchange relation. This is the result of the action and reaction of the closely related and interdependent forces, demand and supply, and the somewhat stable equilibrium established between them in a socially systematic way.

Interest consequently centers in cost, that regulates the movement.

In the same way that consumption is the incentive to and measure of production, cost limits supply; it is the obstacle to be overcome in the creation of wealth. Through price, demand exercises a controlling influence over supply. "Wants, efforts, satisfactions" is the circle of economic activity, but the second step is only the means by which the first motive is actualized in the third condition. Today's wants determine tomorrow's efforts; yesterday's actual consumption determines the direction and extent of today's production. But while demand is thus the cause of supply, a continuous supply will be forthcoming only as demand is strong enough to insure the giving of an economic equivalent for the efforts expended in production.

Demand, not competition, is the life of trade. Demand always means want and consumption, howsoever complex the industrial relations may be; supply means personal service and production. The supply must depend on demand at a price which will equal cost. It is effectual demand that creates price; price induces production; cost limits supply. This is why mankind always lives from hand to mouth and does not produce more than will maintain the normal current in any state of civilization. Production cannot be much in advance of consumption, nor the world's aggregate wealth much in excess of the aggregate wants of the people of the world. Demand is determined by the habitual wants and the social character of the mass of the people. As a consequence, nothing can permanently increase the quantity and reduce the cost of wealth which does not multiply the wants, extend the life, enlarge the consumption, and thus expand the social character of the community.

Supply involves cost. This is the obstacle which price must overcome by equaling it. So long as demand is not correctly anticipated or the utility of an article accurately estimated, industrial fluctuations occur. When the cost level rises so that price does not cover expenditure, loss, failure and bankruptcy ensue. A continuous supply will be maintained only at a price equal to cost.

This does not mean that the price at which each article is sold is determined by the cost of producing that particular article, nor by the average cost of making that kind of an article, but the cost of replacing it. This equals the cost of producing the economic substitute or of producing that portion of the necessary supply which is produced under the greatest disadvantages. Competition forces prices toward cost. When the cost level is so low that a liberal margin of profit exists for all engaged in any enterprise, other labor and capital will be directed toward this channel of production and an equilibrium established on the basis of a price which

equals the cost. Cost is the economic point below
which competition cannot permanently force prices and
above which competition will not permit them to be
maintained. It is therefore the point of equilibrium—
the point at which trade becomes mutually profitable
and permanent because it is an exchange of economic
equivalents.

This is true of agricultural as well as of manufactured products; it applies to trade among barbarians
who are but just beginning to barter within narrow
limits, and, in a more perfect way, to the trade of the
United States with all its variety and complexity. This
explanation of price phenomena accounts for the daily
fluctuations as well as for the average rate of exchange :
they are the result of changes in cost. "No variation
of demand, unaccompanied by a variation in the cost
or real value of commodities, has any lasting influence
over prices."*

Changes in the quantity of goods in a market cannot
affect value save as the increased or diminished supply
is accompanied by a change in cost, or is occasioned by
a forced sale. The price of agricultural products, for
instance, seems to vary with changes in the quantitative
ratio of supply to demand; but it does so because the
change in quantity has entailed a change in the cost
per unit. So evident is this, that farmers are habitually
complaining because they do not get any more for a
large crop, which results from good weather, than they
do for a small one. In truth, the price in each instance
gravitates toward the cost of raising the most expensive
portion marketed, whether the major part of this was produced in America, as in 1889, or in Russia, as in 1892.

Toward the same limit the daily variations are constantly tending. Each day it is known with reasonable
accuracy where every bushel of wheat in existence is

---

* McCulloch, " Principles of Political Economy," Fourth Edition, p. 333.

to be found. The members of boards of trade and of exchanges are constantly estimating the cost of getting the most expensive bushels that will be paid for into the market at a particular place, and make their "contracts to deliver" on the basis of their knowledge of market conditions.

31.—Importance of the Market.

The extent of the market is often an all-important element in determining economic conditions and relations. The sententious phrase of Professor Perry,* "a market for products is products in market," suggests an important truth. It often happens that the condition of success in the adoption of a new method in production is a larger market for the products. But it is entirely outside the province and power of capital to create the conditions of its own successful employment. Otherwise capital would never be idly waiting in hundreds of millions of dollars for profitable investment, and the bankruptcies and industrial depressions which characterize modern industry would be impossible. Capital is a tool, an instrument, a means; and its function is to supply markets, not to create them. Commodities are supplied only because there is a demand for them, not sold because they can be produced; consequently the new capital or improved machinery will be used, steam and electricity will be substituted for muscle, only when it is possible to reduce the cost per unit by marketing the whole of the larger product. As the cost of the whole must be met by the amount sold, the success of a machine which will greatly multiply the output thus depends on selling the increased quantity. Something more than a mere addition to the capital in existence is necessary to make its economic use possible because profitable.

"Principles of Political Economy," p. 185.

Not only is it true that those articles have value for
which alone some one stands ready to give something
in exchange, but it is equally important to note that the
value of a great many commodities at any particular
time and place is due in large measure to the people
who have wants to satisfy and who stand ready to give
an economic equivalent. It may not pay to produce
one hundred, but if ten thousand are required the cost
per unit may be considerably less and the commodity
find a market.

Professor Perry's formula fails to take into full consideration that the tender of service may be quite as
much a market for products as the products themselves,
and that service is all that the vast majority of mankind, the laborers, have to offer. It is because of the
economic relation which wages bear to the extent of
the market, and the extent of the market to price, that
makes the seeming paradox an all-important social
truth, that high wages and low prices are correlative,
and that a rise in the general rate of wages tends to
lower the cost of production per unit of product and
extend the use of machinery. Merely to discharge
laborers is to reduce the market for goods. If the use
of capital involved only their discharge, capitalists
would in truth be the enemies of laborers. But there is
no motive to produce more or to produce more cheaply
if no one buys. It is thus in the new desires and
greater capacities for pleasure that laborers and capitalists find a common interest, the one in higher wages
and the other in wider use for his possessions and the
incentive to increase them.

High wages do not produce lower prices instantane-
ously, however, but through the gradual social effect of
the possible higher standard of living, and the new desires
which are at once the occasion and the means of higher
wages and lower prices. Lowering the cost of produc-

tion through the widening of the market is consequently a slow process requiring large additions to the capital engaged in industry. A particular manufacturer cannot sell at a low price because he pays high wages; but low prices accompany high wages in any community, because high wages imply a widening market and consequently a larger use of the forces of nature.

32.—The Movement of Prices.

The striking fact in the recent history of prices is the decline in the price of manufactured goods. Wages, on the other hand, have pretty regularly increased, and the prices of several agricultural products have risen as much or more than wages have in the present century. Clearly this is not due to changes in the ratio of supply to demand. Manufactured goods are cheaper than ever before, and there are also more of them. But it has never been true for any length of time that there were not laborers in the market seeking employment. Moreover, the disparity between agricultural and hand-made products on the one side and manufactured goods on the other, in the matter of price variation, is greatest in the most highly civilized countries. Quantitative changes do not account for the movement.

Changes in the "visible supply" are readily observed; they are among the things people can see. But in truth they are only the accompanying incidents of price variation; the unrecognized cause is a change in the cost per unit of a considerable portion of the supply. When the change is due to the action of cosmic forces, as is apt to be the case with agricultural products, price and quantity vary inversely; the added supply reduces average cost, so that a cotton crop in 1840 only brings as much on the market as that of 1815, which was one-sixth as large,* and seven leading crops in the United

* See Carey's "Harmony of Interests."

States, as shown by the reports of the Department of Agriculture, can be sold in a scant year (1881) for more money than the same seven crops in an abundant year (1880). Exactly the same result follows the larger use of capital (natural forces) in industry, increase in production being accompanied by a decline in price, because the cost per unit of product has been lowered through the use of new machinery and better organization and consolidation of plant. The production of pig iron has been doubled, but the price reduced one-half, in twenty years. Cost of transportation has been reduced from three cents to three-eighths of a cent per ton mile for freight on the N. Y. C. & H. R. R. R., and from four cents to less than one for passengers. A telegram from New York to Chicago which cost $2.20 in 1866 is sent today for forty cents. While the production has steadily increased, the price of print cloth has declined from seventeen cents per yard to less than three; of steel rails from $158 in 1868 to $26.50 per ton; of crude oil from 9.42 cents per gallon in 1873 to 1.59 cents in 1887, and of refined oil from 23.59 cents to 6¾ cents per gallon in the same period.*

Increased costs come where nature cannot be utilized either directly or through the investment of capital, and where the labor cost has risen because men and women have insisted on the wages necessary to a higher standard of living. The Hoe press, for instance, has made books and papers cheap, although the price of typeseting has more than doubled; but it costs fifty per cent more to build a house in New York today than it did a generation ago, because bricklayers, masons, carpenters and painters all get higher wages, and in this instance machinery cannot be used to any large extent.

As the conclusion of the whole matter we have then

*For further illustration see Report (Senate) Finance Com., March 3, 1893; First Report (U.S.) Bureau of Labor, 1886; Wells, "Recent Economic Changes"; Atkinson, "The Distribution of Products."

the following law of prices,—that is, the statement of the way price-creating forces act at all times and under all conditions: PRICES BOTH OF COMMODITIES AND OF SERVICE TEND TO EQUAL THE COST OF CONTINUOUSLY PRODUCING THE MOST EXPENSIVE PORTION OF THE SUPPLY NECESSARY IN ANY MARKET.

Summary.

1. Demand is the cause of supply,—the active force to which supply is the social response.

2. Demand, to insure a supply, must be at a price equal to the cost of furnishing the dearest portion of the regular supply.

3. Trade is a part of the process of the production of wealth, and to be continuous must be an exchange of economic equivalents.

4. Cost is the point to which competition drives prices, and thus different quantities of various kinds of wealth and service can be exchanged as economic equivalents; they represent the same amount of economic expenditure.

5. Industrial fluctuations are inversely to the degree of economic knowledge and the freedom of economic movement.

6. Cost of production is ultimately determined by the price of labor. High wages usually imply low labor cost.

7. Wealth and service vary inversely in price, progress consisting of a fall in the value of commodities and a rise in the value of labor; that is, the prices of goods decline as wants increase in number and complexity, and as man becomes dear.

www.ingramcontent.com/pod-product-compliance
Lightning Source LLC
Chambersburg PA
CBHW021633270326
41931CB00008B/998